The Future Performer

The Parents Handbook

By
(Kim Thursfield)

Copyright 2024 by Kim Thursfield – All rights reserved.

It is not legal to reproduce, duplicate or transmit any part of this document in either electronic means or printed format. Recording of this publication is strictly prohibited.

This book is dedicated to:	My two daughters Alana & Mila x

Contents

Introduction
Part I: The Early Years
Chapter 1: Finding the Right Class
Chapter Two: Auditions And Agents
Part II: Full Time Stage Schools
Chapter III: How Stage Schools run
Chapter IV: The Audition Process
Chapter V: Further Education
Kim's Singing Tips
Self Tape Tips
A Poem
References
Acknowledgements
About The Author

Introduction

Thank you for purchasing my book. Your guide to a realistic approach to being a young performer, or a parent of a young performer starts here.
'The Future Performer' dives deep into all of the problems that can occur within the performing arts industry. The good and the bad things, the ups and the downs. A child might be born for the stage, but does that mean an expensive stage school is the best solution?

Not every parent is born into the world of performing arts, and may not know where to begin with a child who expresses an interest in performing.
This book will tell you the ins and outs, starting from the early years, all the way through to the teens, speaking from experience as a child that attended Stage School, and as someone who has also seen plenty of children sent to stage schools. We will delve into the extra expenses that can occur, the education side, the travelling, the opportunities and the sadness.

I loved performing from a very young age and I was never very academic. I went to a "normal" school for a year and hated it, so, I was sent to a prestigious stage school at age 12 and I stayed there until I was 18…

This book will guide you through the process of starting stage school, or may even help you decide whether to accept a place or not.

Recently, a young girl I taught singing to, auditioned and received a fee-paying place at a top London Stage School. She was already talented but was failing with her academic side. She's now in Year 9 and her dyslexia has improved since receiving 1-2-1 support that she wouldn't necessarily receive at a state school, full of 200 children in a year.
I was never particularly an academic child, but I definitely would not have received a B in GCSE Maths had I not have attended a Private School with only 22 children in my year.

So read on if you would like a realistic view, the pros and cons to sending your child to Stage School, amongst other things such as agents, auditions and local classes.

The opinions in this book are solely my own and do not express the opinions of others in the industry.

PART I: The Early Years

Your Son or Daughter began singing, acting or dancing at an early age. Why? Because they loved putting on shows at home? Or they were always singing, making up their own songs? Always copying the dance moves from music videos? Or nowadays its 'Tik Tok.' If this is currently your five year old then there's no reason why not to send them to a local dance school.

Most parents of girls start with Ballet. Ballet is great as it not only lets you have plenty of photo opportunities for your child wearing a pretty tutu, but it provides the strength, discipline and technique they need from an early age. There are baby ballet classes around that start from when a baby is sitting up. Admittedly these are more like baby sensory classes at this age.

There are plenty of amazing local Theatre Schools all around. The best way to find one is to ask for local recommendations. It doesn't really matter how many children attend, if there are 40 or 400, all theatre school principals work really hard and are usually ex performers themselves, so they have a lot of creative passion and are usually not in it for the money.

I attended Dance Schools from the age of five. My Parents weren't pushy, I just enjoyed it and I wasn't very sporty. Horse Riding was too far away and too expensive, so performing arts was a good call. I made a lot of friends (Some I'm still in touch with now) because it was fun to look forward to seeing different friends that you do not spend all day with in school. You're with those children all week for 6 hours a day so it's nice to have friends at a different place at the weekend or in the evening.

To sum up, if your child enjoys their dance/drama club, then let them attend for as long as they can. There's no need to move them because you think another school is better because your neighbour Jane said so. If they have friends there and they are happy, there's no need to fix something that is not broken.

Chapter One: Finding the right class

So, your child has shown an interest in performing arts. Maybe they did a workshop at school and really enjoyed it.
Some schools operate one day a week and offer all 3 disciplines (Singing, Acting and Dancing) on rotation. Others have a timetable where you can pick and choose the classes that may be right for your child.

I would always advise not to start singing lessons with children until they can read properly. This is speaking as a Vocal Coach also.
For young children, the classes should be fun and interactive, and still include games. Between the ages of 3-6 is when the child should be having fun, building their confidence, making new friends and learning some new skills. They won't go home and be able to do the splits or belt out a top C, but they might be singing a new song from a Disney film or coming out of class with a smile from ear to ear (but not from head to toe. Sorry for the Annie pun).
Once your child is around age 6/7, you can usually see their strongest discipline whether its singing, acting or dancing.

If dancing is their strength, have a look at dance schools that offer different genres of dance and even dance grades. There is no doubt at all that Modern, Tap and Ballet are the best genres to train in. The grades can be taken with I.S.T.D (Imperial Society Of Teachers Of Dancing), IDTA (International Dance Teachers Association) or RAD (Royal Academy of Dance). There are others, but these are the main ones that are recognised across the UK. With these, children can take examinations which they work towards each year as they go up the grades. The teachers will only put the children forward for exams who they believe are strong enough so DO NOT NAG the teacher if you're child has not been put forward, as they do not want the child to be set up for failure and be disappointed with their results. All children move at different levels. These classes may be quite mixed with ages, as some children will pick things up a lot quicker than others. Please make sure that the dance teachers are fully qualified to teach each discipline. A ballet teacher in particular who isn't qualified can be very dangerous.

On top of this I would also recommend Street Dance classes although exams in this are not needed.

If drama is your child's strength, you can take exams in LAMDA (London Academy Of Music and Dramatic Art). Thinking long term, drama is actually very beneficial. Of course, confidence is key to public speaking. There are many jobs that require speaking publicly, such as a Lecturer, Politician, Presenter, Journalist, Doctor, the list goes on. SO, even if your child may not end up on the stage, drama is a great skill to have for future use. Once you reach a certain grade (6) in LAMDA you can also use points toward your UCAS application.

In singing, there is absolutely no need to take exams. There isn't anything you can do in a singing exam that a regular singing teacher won't teach you. If you walk into a West End Audition with your Grade eight in singing they do not care. If you can sing to the high standard that they require then that's all they need.

As a vocal coach, I do not teach singing exams. I had a student I taught for about 3 years who did not play an instrument. He still decided to take Music as a GCSE and used his voice in his practical exam. I was even lucky enough for him to ask me to sing with him as his Duet, so we worked on harmonies etc. He received an A at GCSE level and this student is now finishing his A levels and begins his Degree in Drama at University this year.

That being said, there are some singing examination courses that can offer UCAS points also, and it can help with reading music which is a really handy skill to have.

Children who are West End standard that I have taught, do not take singing exams. We study audition technique in class and work on their voice and repertoire. They are either right or wrong for a part but the audition panel certainly do not care if they have their grades.

Of course with taking examinations, comes extra costs. Uniform must be correct, dance shoes, exam fees and extra coaching. Be prepared to spend this if you would like your child to take regular exams in Dance/Drama.

If you would prefer your child not to take exams, then sticking with a fun dance school is fine. I used to run a franchise Theatre school of my own. It ran on Saturday mornings and most children stayed from an early age until they started secondary school. I watched confidence grow, friendships made and lots of smiles. There were no competitions or exams, just fun and the children would learn new songs and dances every week.
I wouldn't necessarily pick a school that has a "Celebrity" name attached to it. The celebrity is never usually there and is just running it as a side business, and it's usually to gain more publicity for themselves.

It also doesn't matter if you choose a school that has its own studios or one that hires a primary school or a church hall. The teachers will still be the same standard and costs would probably be lower at a school that doesn't own it's own premises.
At the end of the day, sometimes it's not about the dance school you choose, but the teachers who are there. You could go to a dance school with 10 children but the teacher might be amazing and will teach the same thing that a school with 400 children does.
Of course, make sure the teachers have a DBS check, first aid and public liability insurance. You are leaving them in charge of your children.

Drama and singing helped me throughout Primary School. In year five or six, I was part of the school choir. They never really did solos back then at school, it was all about being a group, but I remember singing at care homes and putting on little concerts for the elderly. The choir teacher asked me to introduce each song as I had the loudest and clearest voice.
Workshops are also a great way to gain experience, but make sure you continue with the regular lessons too.

I would also recommend learning to play an instrument from a young age. This can help with rhythm, reading music and prepares them for taking exams. Once they go to Secondary school they can even join the Orchestra. Of course it's another expense to think about.

Show Time

Most Theatre Schools big or small will put on a show either at the end of each term, or a big show at the end of the year.

This was always the highlight for me from an early age. Performing on a big stage, feeling tired the next day, the costumes, the makeup and the buzz of eating in the dressing room with all of your friends.

Parents be prepared for extra costs! Costumes cost money. You may have to buy them outright or rent them from the school owner. Yes they could just do a show without costumes, but then your child wouldn't have that experience of dressing up and becoming a character on stage, or having a quick change in the wings in just two minutes. They look amazing on stage with the lights etc then you will get the photos and in turn, keep those memories forever too.

Tickets will also cost money. The dance school owner is renting out a huge Theatre. They are paying staff, music licenses and not to mention their time and effort that goes into the planning, so they need to make their money back via the ticket sales. SO invite Grandparents, aunties, neighbours, whoever will go and watch, your child will love it knowing they are performing for lots of people. The show may go on late and it may be on a school night. Don't moan about this. It's one night out of a whole year and yes your child might be tired but they will have had an amazing time.

If you're particularly worried, speak to your local council about becoming a volunteer Chaperone. Your licence will last for three years and you can help backstage. It's only a three hour course and its free! You will also have to undergo a DBS check.

The experience of performing in a show is not one you can gain from just doing classes. From all of the backstage antics, putting on makeup, staying up late, quick changes and tech runs; being on the stage really helps gain confidence and learn how to actually perform, not just dance.

It's also a good idea to look for local opportunities such as Pantomimes and Amateur Dramatics. All stage opportunities are good opportunities and help with confidence and experience, both backstage and on stage.

Favouritism

Ok, favouritism can be a thing when it comes to the shows. It's not due to your child being rubbish, it's just that usually the same children get solo parts or get to be in the front centre of a dance routine because they are just really good! Whilst the shows are all about all children being seen and you don't want to buy tickets to watch other peoples children, they are also about showcasing these children who show true passion and can make the number look or sound amazing.

If a child with an amazing voice at age seven gets a one line solo, within another year their voice has grown stronger, so they should still be heard because if they're working hard then they are only going to get better and better.

The same for a child that is a very strong dancer. They will only get stronger if they keep working, which is why it's usually the same child at the front all the time. Your child may also be getting stronger each year but they will always be slightly behind the other child, or maybe they are just dancing because they just love it and don't want to be at the front in the limelight.

If your child is the child at the front or getting to sing the whole solo to themselves, then perhaps it is your child that may want to go to stage school.

As a Singing teacher myself, I love to try and give everyone a chance in a show. If a child has been attending my classes for three years and has simply become confident and are happy and willing to do a solo, then I love to give them a chance. It makes them even more confident and gives them something to boast about at school.

Chapter Summary/Key Takeaways

In a nut shell, not all children are destined to be professional performers, but even still, performing arts is great for all children and can help them learn essential life skills.

In the next chapter, you will learn…

More about auditions for TV, Film and Theatre and finding the right agent.

Chapter Two: Auditions & Agents

Your child is now aged between nine and ten, and they are showing amazing progress in their Theatre classes. Before we talk about stage schools in the second part of the book, lets talk about auditions and agents!

Auditions

When I was a child, I only ever had one big audition for a West End Show. Back then it was "Whistle Down The Wind." I sang 'Happy Birthday' and was cut off after two lines. I also actually auditioned to be a student in the Harry Potter films but didn't quite make the cut. Child performers weren't really a thing apart from in TV & Film. Fast forward to current times and we have Matilda, School Of Rock, Annie and much more, all making it very accessible for talented children to perform professionally on a West End Stage or tour. I'll be honest, these auditions are grueling! There are usually about five different rounds to go through along with call backs, cuts, long days and waiting for weeks for an email.

The children who are in these shows really are the best of the best! There is absolutely no point in sending your child if they cannot sing confidently or pick up a routine. Both you and the child need to be quite thick skinned.

The castings for these shows are also very precise. If the casting mentions their height must be under 4"4 then that is exactly what it should be! They will not see your child if they are 4"5 but an amazing singer. It wastes their time and yours and believe me they do get the measuring tape out. The same thing stands if the casting says aged between nine and 12, there is no point in sending your eight year old. They wouldn't be within licence requirements anyway! (More on that later).

For Matilda dancers, especially as they have to be Grade four and above in their dance grades, please don't go through the heartache of sending your grade 2 child or a child with no grades at all, it will simply cause heartache when they can't pick up the routine and feel like they've failed.

Auditions can be horrible for a child's mental health, especially if they get a lot of 'no's.' It is definitely worth speaking to their drama, dance, singing teacher or agent to make sure they agree that your child is strong enough to go to the audition. That being said, rejection at an early age does help set them up for the future. Not just in this industry, but in any.

Not only is there the stage for young performers, but TV and Film is also calling out for children. Every soap needs children, every Netflix series and of course commercials.

All Auditions are completely different. Some will have five or six rounds and others may only have two. Be aware of everyone around you at auditions, try not to bad mouth anyone as the runner or a Chaperone can feedback to the Casting Directors and they definitely won't want to work with rude parents. Try not to ask too many questions, (your agent will know the answer anyway). Children also need to be on their best behaviour. A Chaperone will always report back as to whether a child is well behaved or not as unfortunately they do not want challenging children backstage or on set as it is a working environment.

You should never pay to attend an audition; this is a well known scam. The only thing you need to pay for is any travel.

Try not to nag your agent after the audition about when you will hear. You may not hear anything at all. Try not to ask about other children on their books as this can go against their GDPR policy.

Be Prepared!

For some auditions they will send you the material they want you to sing/dance or read. Others will ask you to prepare your own song or monologue. Do not let your child walk into an audition unprepared. They should know their song and monologue or poem off by heart.

Do not dress your child in tiny shorts and a belly top. They need to be dressed as a child. I always recommend a bright coloured top (no logos) and leggings and of course the correct shoes for dancing. They do not need to dress up as the part they are going for i.e Matilda, Anna, Elsa etc. No makeup and hair neatly tied back.

Your child must be able to take on direction. If the Director or Casting Director asks them to perform their song or monologue in a different way, they must be able to correct themselves. At the end of the day if the child gets the job, they need to go to rehearsals and be able to listen well and take on their corrections. If they have worked with a Singing/Drama/Dance teacher on their audition piece, they still need to be able to understand a Directors instructions and not revert back to their old way of doing things. This is why sometimes they will ask children not to work on their prep, so they come into the audition room with a more natural approach.

A Director will not want to work with them if they are chatting too much, do not take on board corrections, or if they think they are unable to be in a team of children. A company does not want to be dealing with bullying accusations whilst on tour or in the West End.

Self Tapes
Thanks to the Coronavirus we are now in an era where most auditions (especially for TV & Film) are done via self tape first.
Always think of a self tape as a serious audition, not just something you can easily do at home for a bit of fun.
Self tapes should be shot landscape against a plain, neutral background and not in a bedroom or whilst sat on the toilet. They should not be holding a script as they are looking down and therefore cannot see their eyes. They shouldn't be wearing a onesie or their football outfit (unless they specifically ask for this). And not with granny in the background or with lots of noise. Imagine a Casting Director receiving the self tape and then watching it on a TV screen. This is how they see who looks best on camera.
Again, with a self tape they still need to be prepared. They should learn the material off by heart. Sometimes the turnarounds for self tapes can be very quick, within 24 hours. My advice is to get it done as soon as possible rather than leaving it until the last minute. Don't be disheartened if your agent asks you to redo a self tape. They just want you to have the best possible chance. Remember, no jobs for you also means no commission for the agent.
I would also recommend getting your tape to your agent sooner than the deadline that is given. This will allow time to redo it if your agent asks you to,

and also allows the casting director extra time to view your tape before others come in.

A slate is also referred to as an ident. This is simply your neutral accent to the camera saying your name, age/DOB, height and location. This can sometimes be filmed in portrait if they request it, so they can see the whole body. They may also ask to see the front and back of your hands, and the profiles of your face (each side).

Also see Kim's Self Tape tips.

Recalls

Recalls should be shouted about! It's still such an achievement to get through a first round, second round or even make it to a seventh round for some auditions! Obviously it can be really gutting to make it to the final and then not get the part, in a way it's much better to go out in the first round.

Casting Directors will quite often never give feedback! This may be because your child simply isn't right for the part and never will be. They might be too tall, too thin, too cockney, too tired or they simply do not fit with the rest of the team/children that have been selected. Sometimes it can be best not to know the answer because it may actually not be want you want to hear, and this is why feedback is often not given.

Casting Directors will also let you know if they want to see your child in the future. If they do not want to see them, there simply isn't anything that can be done and it's best to move on to something else. This isn't the agents fault and it really is disappointing for them too.

Unfortunately there are some occasions where you just don't hear anything. It's quite refreshing to receive an email from the Casting Director to say "It hasn't gone in your direction" because at least you can move on and not have to think about that one anymore. It can be frustrating to not receive anything at all but this is quite common, particularly with commercials and first stage self tapes.

Pencils

Pencils mainly occur with commercials. It's when the Casting team/Director will pencil around 10-20 children for the one job and even licence them all.

This means, you must essentially 'pencil' the date/s for the shoot and keep them free. They will eventually only confirm one child and sometimes they do not even let the others know that they are no longer required. Someone I know has been on a pencil since 2007. It's still a positive as it means that out of hundreds of children, they still really liked you and it's a step further towards confirming a job.

Finding the right Agent

I'm writing this as an agent myself, but I've been a performer and I have known plenty of children and adults sign with the wrong agent.
Firstly, let's talk about modelling agents. These are very different to Talent agents and I myself am not a modelling agent. You must decide whether your child wants to pursue a career in modelling or performing because they are very different.
You must be extremely careful with modelling agencies because there are so many scams out there. Every parent thinks that their child is beautiful, and these scam agents like to use this to their advantage.
They will offer you a portfolio package where you spend £200 upwards for a lovely photoshoot of your child that they can then use to put forward for other agents. Modelling agencies are legally not allowed to ask for fees to join so the way they get around this is to provide a portfolio. There is also no such thing as a casting agent! There are agents and there are Casting Directors, there is no in-between.

There are of course fees that should be taken into consideration. Children do need photos but these are done by outside companies not the agency itself. Most agents will have a recommended list of headshot photographers. A modelling agency will require specific model photos, a talent agency will require headshots.
Headshots are literally that. Head and shoulder images that look as natural as possible. No makeup, no jewellery, no logos and hair completely natural. They should look exactly like you would, if you were to walk into an audition.

The other cost is spotlight. Spotlight is the premier casting platform for all actors and performers. This is what all agents will use to submit clients for any castings that come through. It's an online CV where all credits can be added along with headshots and video footage showreel.

You do not need to spend a huge amount on a showreel, if anything at all. Children are different to adults and a simple song, monologue and introduction/slate is sufficient for a casting director to be able to see if they fit the casting requirements. Show off your child's personality. It doesn't need to be a robotic like introduction, they can talk about their hobbies and interests. One child of mine actually got a job because in her video she said she hated her sister!

Keep Spotlight updated with new skills and training too. Even if your child can swim or play tennis, that's an extra skill that can be added.

Casting Directors can also search on Spotlight and filter exactly what they are looking for. For example, Female, Blonde hair, Blue eyes, Plays football, age 9, located in London. Then all of the suggestions would appear and they will ask the agents for availability and in turn, ask to audition. It's worth noting that a young performer cannot have a spotlight profile without an agent. An adult can.

There are other platforms such as "Mandy" and "Star Now', but the castings on these seem to be much smaller and a lot of non professionals are able to use them. They therefore may not know about safeguarding and performance licences. Agents will not use these as it's not worth their time and sometimes the castings are just duplicates.

All agents will accept new applications differently. Some will hold audition days, others will ask for self tapes or a zoom meeting. They are interviewing both the child as much as the parent as they want to make sure they can work with you both. Try to follow the instructions on how to apply to them, I personally can't stand receiving messages on Instagram!

Your agent is the one submitting the clients for the castings they think they are suitable for. The Casting Director is the one who decides if they are seen or not.

Obviously there has to be a good relationship between you and the agent, perhaps you'd rather your child didn't tour or go abroad, therefore the agent wouldn't submit for those roles. You should also make sure you tell your agent any dates you're unavailable or going on holiday so that the agent isn't submitting for any roles that may clash in this timeframe. Make sure you communicate and always let your agent know if you're on holiday. There is nothing worse than submitting for a great job only to find out you're on a beach in The Maldives! Always keep your child's height up to date, children grow all the time and the agent doesn't want to waste anyone's time by submitting for a casting where the height limit is 4"11 but your child is now actually 5"1. Obviously, the agent will want to work very hard as they earn their money through commission. So if your child gets a job, then they will take their commission from this. The usual fees can be anywhere form 10% - 35%.
My advice would be to sign with an agent that has industry experience. There are some agents that set up agencies as a business but without any actual knowledge of the industry itself. Do your research. It's worth noting that agents will not just take anyone on, it simply isn't in their interest for children not to work.

Do be prepared for your child to miss school. Depending on the job they may have a tutor on set with them. It's always good to have your school on side though, be transparent with them and keep your child's attendance as high as possible.

Auditions can take place any time and sometimes will only give you 24 hours notice. A lot of the castings will take place in London or now via self tape or zoom so make sure you are available at the right time. It can sometimes be a juggle with work. And and sometimes it may be required to take a day off school (although most will be after school). If you work full time, this may not be suitable for you so do make sure you think about these things before signing with an agent as repeatedly turning down auditions can be very frustrating, especially if they are pushing for your child to be seen and keeping a good relationship with casting directors.

There are two different types of agencies: sole and non sole.

A sole agency means you are solely represented by them and cannot have another agent. Sometimes they may allow you to have a separate agent just for modelling so long as they are your sole representation for all theatre, tv and film jobs.

Non sole means you can have more than one agent. Some people have four different non sole agents. This can be good and perhaps mean more castings but it is also confusing for casting directors who may receive four different submissions via spotlight for the same child for the same job. It takes up a lot of their time having to go through all of their submissions, so if they have four of the same child it can be an annoyance for them.

Be aware that most agents receive the same briefs for all jobs. Any that you may see on Facebook are usually the same ones that your agent will have already received first. Agents are not permitted to post spotlight breakdowns on their social media feeds unless specifically asked by the casting director.

I would also like to point out that once a tape has been viewed by a casting director they then shortlist the tapes for the main Director. It's then down to that main Director on who they choose.

Us agents have a term for those that like to try different agents -"Flip floppers!" They will flop from agent to agent because they think the grass will be greener elsewhere.

Unfortunately, there are some children who will join an agency and not receive a single audition. This may not be the agents fault, the child may be submitted for castings but never chosen to tape or audition. Other children might receive an audition once a month or even once a week, it really depends on their casting type.

Some Agents use a system called "Tagmin" which enables you to view all the submissions that your agent has been sending. If your agent does not use Tagmin, you can always ask to see a list of submissions. It does take 24 hours for these submissions to populate on Tagmin. So please wait until the day after a job is posted before chasing up. Chances are, your child has already been submitted if they are right for the role.

So, in short a casting will be posted. All agents will submit for the casting. The Casting Director may get more than 1000 submissions depending on the job. The Casting Director will then shortlist down to say 100 to audition or self tape. From there the Casting Director will then choose the best 25-50 to show the Director and the Director will ask who to recall. Auditions are very important, and self tapes are too in order to make a good impression.

I also have to give a shout out now to The AYPA (Agents Of Young Performers Association) which was formed in 2022 to fight for a better standard in the industry and keep children safe. I have been a member from the beginning and we are starting to see the benefit in the industry. AYPA members have a code of conduct to stick to which is available on their website. There is power in numbers!

I would recommend finding an agent whilst your child is young. Unfortunately the work can dry up once they hit age 13+, unless your teenager is tiny and looks like a 10 year old. It is preferred for a 16 year old (Out of licence) to play a 14 year old. They simply have the maturity and there is less risk than hiring a child. I have had many a parent come to me with a very talented teenager who can sing and dance etc but unfortunately, they are too tall and have hit puberty. The best thing to do at this stage is to carry on getting the best training possible and look at 16+ opportunities.
The best time to find an agent is around eight years old and hopefully stay with them and gain opportunities with them.

Agents shouldn't really enforce a termination clause. If a client wishes to leave and has found another reputable agent, then they are free to leave with immediate effect, and shouldn't be tied into staying with their current agent for one month or more. The previous agent will then send on a "protected list" to the new agency which secures any previous submissions to them. An agent however, can offer a one month clause if they are removing the client from their books. This gives them time to find a new agent whilst still having their spotlight profile active. Once a new agent has been found, they will then send on the protected list to the new agent. If you have a current job with the previous agent, the commission and any dealings with contracts etc will still be with the previous agent. If you are thinking of moving agencies, do try and have an open and honest discussion with your current agent. There's nothing worse than finding out via the new agent or just having them disappear from spotlight. It can be very hurtful when we have put lots of effort into gaining auditions and experience for a client who is ready to jump ship at any given moment. I guess this can happen in most industries, but I think it shows how much we care.

I personally love guiding my clients through their own personal journey. One young boy came to me at age eight for singing lessons and I knew straight away where his career would go. He's now 12 and is just finishing his fifth West End show! Once he hits puberty and his voice breaks we can have a look into Television and Film Opportunities as he will have already had a lot of experience behind him. Unfortunately this doesn't just happen for everyone. There is a lot of "Right place, right time" and also the right kind of child and parent. This particular parent is not pushy, plays everything by ear and is quite happy to have a break.
An eight year old would be great gaining experience even just from auditioning, before hitting the age of nine when they can work for longer hours and do West End/Shows. They might even be lucky enough to secure a commercial or small TV part which can then go on their Spotlight CV as a credit.

A small part of being an agent is taking a risk.
A parent contacted me back in 2018 when I was first starting out and they lived in Ireland. They sent me tapes of their very talented actress who was eight years old, but I wasn't sure if I would be any good for them as I was London based and had no contacts in Ireland. I turned them down initially. A couple of weeks later I had a job come through for a commercial for an Irish child and I then contacted them again to see if they would be interested and they were asked to audition straight away. They didn't get the job but a few years later and she is playing the lead in a TV series. Perseverance is key. Trust your agent.

Try not to choose an agent based on what you read on Facebook groups or the number of followers on Instagram. An agent won't always shout about jobs they have secured on their social media pages as they may be under an NDA

(Non Disclosure Agreement) and therefore can't publicise it until they are allowed to do so.

Agents can wear many hats and do a lot more than you may think including:
- Searching and submitting for jobs
- Scouting new talent
- Reading Scripts
- Organising/editing self tapes
- Attending events/shows
- Keeping up to date with current clients
- Posting on social media
- Networking
- Going through contracts

And various other things along with acting as a councillor/friend to clients too.

Child Performance Licence

All children who have not completed their GCSE's must have a licence to perform publicly whether on stage, TV or modelling. This is usually organised via your Agent or Production and will require a form to be filled in for your local council, along with a letter from School (If they are missing School), a photo and birth Certificate. You do not need to pay for this but it is a legal requirement. You and/or the Production company can be fined if you do not follow these legal regulations. It is worth noting, there is no such thing as 'an open licence.' Every job must be licenced on an individual basis.

When is a licence needed:

- the child receives payment for the performance.
- the performance requires absence from school, even if the assignment is unpaid.
- the performance is taking place at a licensed premises or registered club

- the performance is to be broadcast or recorded by whatever means with a view to its use in a future broadcast or film intended for public exhibition.
- a licence is not required if the performance is unpaid, no school absence is required, the performance lasts for four days or fewer and the child has not performed within the previous six months.

More Information

- The age of a child restricts the number of hours they can be on set and breaks needed.
- If schools believe time out will have a negative impact on the child's progress at school, they are able to decline the request. If schools believe that a child's education will suffer as a result of taking part in the performance, they must produce a written statement with evidence to this effect.
- The child must be chaperoned at all times. This may be by the child's own parent or by a registered chaperone hired by the applicant.
- Night work is considered on a case-by-case basis.
- Section 23 of the Children and Young Persons Act 1933 states it is an offence for any person to allow a child under school leaving age to take part in a performance endangering life or limb. A performance of a dangerous nature includes all acrobatic performances and all performances as a contortionist.

Information correct as of 2024, all guidance is subject to change.

KTTA – Frequently asked questions

How do I apply?
Adults must send their Spotlight link and a good Covering letter to be considered.
Young performers please email a CV, Photo and a self tape of them singing, acting or both!
Adults looking for representation please email a covering letter and your Spotlight CV to be considered. Please do not send attachments.

Young Performers looking for representation, please email a CV, photo and a self tape showing acting or singing or both!
If you have had no response within 4 weeks please assume you have been unsuccessful. Unfortunately we do get a lot of representation requests and we cannot respond to everyone.

How does the agency work?

We are a very selective agency so not everyone who applies will be taken on unfortunately. We are not a modelling agency so the agency is very much based on talent.
Children should be able to take direction well and have confidence. Parents should be responsive to messages and have clear communication.
We keep our client base small to be able to focus more on each client individually and build up a more personal relationship with each client.

How much does it cost to join?

KTTA works on commission. (12.5% for children and 15.5% for adults).
That said, there are some costs which all actors should expect to pay in order to have a good chance of work.

Although it's technically possible to represent clients without professional head shots and without a listing in Spotlight, realistically it is very hard to secure appointments for clients without them.
It's an incredibly competitive market, and casting directors often find the talent they need exclusively on Spotlight and don't need to look any further.

We recommend that all our clients pay for a listing in The Spotlight. This currently costs £103 per year for children and £154 for adults. (Adults can pay this monthly by Direct Debit) and young performers can also after being a member for one year.

Clients also require professional head shots which we are able to arrange with our photographer Nancy Collins for around £65 per year. (These prices are for young performers only).

What is Spotlight?
Spotlight is the Premier Casting Platform for young performers and adults in the Performing Arts Industry. It showcases your CV online to Casting Directors.
Young Performers do not have to be on Spotlight prior to joining the agency, we can do this together.
Adults over 25 should already be on Spotlight to be considered.

Do you accept everyone on your books?
No. We are a small agency, we open our books twice a year. We only accept Children and Adults who we truly believe will get Professional work.

Will my child have to miss school?
Almost all professional work involves some time off school/college; production schedules don't fit neatly into weekends or school holidays, so unfortunately it's not possible to represent clients who are unavailable during term time.
Under 16's have to be licensed by their local education authority before they are allowed to perform; as part of this process the school will be asked to grant permission for the time off, and a tutor will be provided by the production company if required. It's important that your school and headteacher are supportive of your child's acting career.

Can you guarantee work for your clients?
Like any agency, we can't guarantee work for our clients; neither can we guarantee auditions!
We receive casting breakdowns every day, and we suggest our clients for all the roles that they are suitable for. However there are many, many young people looking for acting work today, and only a limited number of appointments. For this reason, we ask that clients let us know in advance if they are going to be unavailable for castings or filming.
Please note, children will only be submitted for jobs that they are suitable for. There are height limits for a reason and i am unable to help anyone who is too tall.

How much notice will you give us of auditions?
Typically casting directors give us appointments for castings the following day. This means that we usually contact clients with about 24 hours notice. As appointments are limited, it's essential that you let us know if you are unavailable in advance!

Adult appointments are usually during the daytime, and we may be given less than 24 hours notice, so it's important that you are always contactable, and that you inform us of any work shifts or college commitments which might prevent you from getting to castings.

Where do jobs take place?
A lot of the work we handle takes place in London or around the south east of England, however as the UK is a world leader in the creative industries, we regularly work on projects which take place abroad. We also regularly work on touring theatre productions, and on TV/Film shoots which film on location across the UK.

Can I be represented by more than one agency?
Like most agencies, we insist on having sole representation of our clients, and ask that all work offers are directed to us. The reason for this is that we need to be certain that we know exactly when our clients are available for work, and which jobs they are booked on.

If an actor is represented by two different agencies, they could end up being booked for two different jobs on the same day, which would be disastrous! Likewise, if you're approached directly about a job, please refer it to us- we need to ensure that the correct fees are paid, that child performance regulations are being adhered to; and it may be a job that we have previous declined, as we have concerns about it.

You are welcome to join a modelling agency but it must be for Stills only. You may also have a separate Voiceover agent.

Do you handle modelling work?
Our primary focus is drama work, although we do also work on modelling and catwalk jobs from time to time; generally when the producers are looking for specific performance skills in addition to the right 'look'. If your main interest is

in modelling rather than drama, you may be better off applying to a specialist modelling agency, as the acting and modelling industries are quite different things.

I live a long way from London – should I apply?

We have represented clients from across the UK, and even overseas. So it's certainly possible to be represented by a London agent even if you don't live near the capital. However you should bear in mind that producers will often consider talent with London agents to be 'London based', and won't make any allowances for the additional time and expense involved in getting to auditions. Commercials cast in the south-east may not provide accommodation for talent based further afield, so you may need to arrange for somewhere local to stay the night before the shoot.

That said, self taping is increasingly becoming the norm for the first stage of the casting process, meaning that you can send a video to the casting director in the first instance, and only travel to London if you are brought through to the second round. See "What is a self tape?" for more information.

What is a Self Tape, and how do I make one?

It's increasingly common for casting directors to ask actors to 'self tape' for a role instead of bringing them in for an initial meeting with an assistant. This means filming yourself reading the lines, using a smart phone or tablet (though a DSLR or video camera is fine if you have one).

If they like what they see on the tape, they will then bring the actor in to meet in person, or sometimes bring them straight in for a meeting with the director. This is a good thing, as it means that many more actors get a chance to be considered for a role than would be possible with traditional first round meetings. It also saves you the time and expense of travelling into central London for a role that you might not be quite right for.

You should only send videos to us; please don't upload them yourself to YouTube or similar. In many cases the script that you are asked to film is confidential, and it's important that it doesn't get leaked out to the public. Here are a few more tips and suggestions on self taping from a casting director.

What Should I be doing regularly?

Always keep us up to date with height, availability and skills. Adults if you change your hair or appearance, please let us know. If you get new headshots, keep us informed. If you get any other work yourself or attend other open auditions, let us know. We are proud to work with our clients and would love to showcase your skills.

Also keep up to date with training and skills. Have songs prepared, monologues prepared and stay up to date with industry knowledge.

How do we update availability?
We use a system called TAGMIN so any holiday dates etc can be input in this and will notify us so you are not put forward for anything that may clash. Child clients should also be regularly updating their height measurements.

From a parent's perspective

"Where to start…..I think we had a pretty unconventional entrance in to the industry after discovering my little one could sing during lockdown (he had no background in performing arts). After being continually told I should "do something with his voice" I started the search for a local singing teacher, really just for a bit of fun. Kim's name came up consistently as the go to person and I arranged a lesson. Kim had her own agency (KTTA) and suggested that he would do well in the industry. Initially I wasn't sure, but went for it and it snowballed from there. Kim has been beyond supportive and although one of the smaller agencies this hasn't had any impact on opportunities, with 4 West End Shows (one of which was filmed and released), a National Theatre show, a performance on the final of BGT 2023 and a performance at Downing Street.

It's a tough industry, and brutal at times. It's also a huge commitment for the parents as well as the children, which is something that I hadn't forethought. Auditions, recalls and rehearsals are dates set in stone often with very little notice. Rehearsals periods can be intense and exhausting, as are a lot of show schedules. You can't take holidays during a contract, and the shows we've done have specified that you need to be always an hour or less from London. Being a single mum with a full time job added another layer of complexity, but luckily my work were very supportive and allowed lots of remote working. Another thing I noticed very quickly was that it's expensive! Trying to make sure your child is fed before going in to the theatre when you work full time often results in grabbing a quick bite to eat in London…….what with that, travel costs and the cost of tickets, not to mention all the show merchandise that they "need", it sometimes feels like you're paying for your child to be in a show. All that being said, I wouldn't change a single thing. Seeing him with the other children, adult cast, chaperones, production, WHAM (wig, hair and makeup) and creatives is joyful. He's learnt so much over the last 2.5 years, not just dancing, singing and acting but life skills that he wouldn't have had if he hadn't had this experience. However, the icing on the cake is seeing them up on the big stage living their best life……the pride is indescribable. We have also both made friends for life." – **Parent of a young performer**

From a young performers perspective

Being a child actor is a tough but very rewarding job. Every job starts with an audition. It can be hard when you don't know much about the character but try to understand as much as you can. When going to an audition you can feel nervous but also excited.

My number one tip is being prepared. Know your lines and understand the scene as best you can with limited information. This means understanding how the characters in the scene are feeling and their motives.

When doing a self tape or a face to face audition show your confidence and give it everything, that's all anyone can ask of you.

The days and weeks that follow can be nerve wrecking. Unfortunately most of the time it's silence and the silence can be deafening. You can't be negative, you have to keep going and hoping. My best advice is do the audition / self tape, submit and forget about it as its now in the laps of the Gods!!

"Rejection is just redirection"

But I promise one day you will get that call. The best feeling in the world!! You've got the job and the day arrives. Like any other professional job it can be tough but rewarding. You pack your bags, script and all and off you go with a sense of excitement and nervousness all in one.

Your days can start very early. You usually start your day with rehearsals next is costume and then hair and makeup. Then you spend the rest of your day going between filming and tuition (school).It can be hard switching between your character and yourself so quick.

After a long and hard day you go home, eat, sleep and do it all again tomorrow. Once you finish that job the ball starts rolling all over again........ Auditions, Self-Tapes etc.

However..... It is the most incredible job in the world and I love it!!!!

Kiri Flaherty – **Young performer**

PART II: Full Time Stage Schools

When thinking about secondary school, it may have crossed your mind about sending your child to a full time stage school.
Firstly they have to audition. This may be in year six if you would like them to join in year seven, but most stage schools will allow a child to join in any year. In my own experience, I went to a 'normal' secondary school in year seven and I hated it. I auditioned for a London Stage School and was offered a place for year eight where I stayed until I was 18.
The only issue with stage schools is that in most cases you will have to pay and it's very expensive! If you were thinking of sending your child to a private school anyway, then you may be fine.
Of course if your child is extremely talented and you're on a low income, there are separate auditions for scholarships.
There are other fees to consider also such as clothing, books and travel fees which are also quite hefty depending on where you are travelling from. Then there are added extras for show costumes, exams etc.
My parents had to remortgage their house and make extreme cut backs and it goes without saying I am truly grateful.

Overall, you are also looking at your child's education and essentially a stage school is a private school so the tuition is also supposedly better.
When I was there, there were only nine children in the whole year in year eight! That then grew to 20 children by year 11. This meant that the teachers could work more closely with us. At a normal state school I was failing miserably in Maths but thanks to stage school Maths was my highest GCSE!
The only downside was that we didn't get to choose which GCSE's to take. We took eight but had I have stayed at state school, I definitely wouldn't have taken History! I also loved languages but couldn't take this at Stage school. I was also forced to take Art! I'm a performer so my creative side definitely appeared in my singing and dancing skills and certainly not in Art!
Being a fee paying school, there were also children in my year who were extremely bright and obviously there for the school to have good grade records. I say this because they certainly couldn't sing, act or dance but they were great at Art and got A star grades at GCSE. A parent recently mentioned to me that

due to financial struggles they are having to move their Year nine child currently at Stage School to a State Secondary School and they are concerned because she has never done a Geography lesson.

Chapter Three: How Stage Schools run

So, a typical day at a stage school. We would arrive in the morning in our school uniform and work from 9am – midday on our school studies. Then at lunchtime we would change into our dance wear and work from 1pm – 4pm on our dance, drama, singing etc.

I know another school works so that Monday, Tuesday and Wednesday are school studies only, and Thursdays and Fridays are vocational studies.

Be aware that the day can be a lot longer at a Stage school rather than a state school. Some days were longer than others and I remember not being home until gone 7pm some days and being on a train the next day at 7am.

Travelling to and from London was also a big step, most children will just get the bus to and from their local secondary school but I was travelling by train and tube although I did find friends who were local and travelled with them.

The Stage School I was at also had an agency attached to it, so if you were lucky you would be put forward for jobs and auditions there too. I think I had a grand total of two auditions the whole time I was there!

Whilst at Stage School I also carried on training at the weekend with my local stage school. For some reason the whole time I was at Stage school I didn't take a single dance or drama exam! I carried on and did this elsewhere, which was of course more money for my parents.

Negative Moments

For me a huge negative point was not being a normal teenager. Being in a year of 20 kids they didn't all live in Bromley and came from all over the place. I missed out on going to the local shopping centre at the weekend or hanging out at the park or just calling your friend and going to their house because my best friend there lived in Woking.

Another side effect was that being a normal teenager, you go through hormonal changes. At Stage school there were girls who had perfect skin and hair, and looked like they hadn't eaten in months. I was never a skinny frame and I had breakouts of acne. Looking back now, I realise I definitely had some kind of eating disorder which if I'm honest still hits me now with my relationship with food and my body. I remember trying all sorts of diets and at 16 I was probably the tiniest I had ever been. A dance teacher there actually once said to me "*You have a voice for the radio.*" And she didn't mean I'd be a great radio presenter! She meant I didn't look right body wise and so I shouldn't be seen when singing! I mean as a teacher myself now I would never dream of saying anything like that to a child.

I know of people who are well into their 30's and have been battling with an eating disorder since their teen years. I know of other girls from the school that were hospitalised during college and couldn't complete their final year.
Mental Health definitely wasn't a thing back in the noughties and teachers certainly didn't care if you were anxious or depressed, you just got on with it. That's probably why there's so many problems now. I do believe you have to have a very thick skin to be in this industry, so I guess some of the teachers were trying to prepare you for this (in their own weird way).

Thankfully there has been some impactful changes in recent years focusing on mental health, representation and safeguarding, however I believe that we should still be striving for more change.

Chapter Four: The Audition Process

Each stage school will have their own audition process. Some will ask the child to prepare their own song, dance and acting piece and others will offer a selection of songs to choose from, along with a dance to learn (possibly part of a workshop) and a monologue, sometimes contemporary and classical. They may also interview your child and yourself as part of the process to make sure you are the right fit for the school. Believe it or not, Stage Schools don't just accept anyone, even if they have the money. They want to know that your child is serious and will work hard. They can even ask for an attendance record from a previous school and any reports.

If you are applying for funding, be prepared for them to ask for financial records and proof of income/expenditure.

Ask for help with the audition from your local dance school/Singing/Acting Teacher. This is a big step and they will want to help. Having a child at a full-time stage school is also a great achievement for them.

Chapter Five: Further Education

Whether your child went to a full time stage school, state school or home educated, once they reach 16 they can move onto something else.

Perhaps your child went to Stage School but then decided they wanted to be more academic and move into sixthth form or College. That's ok and they can always continue with their local classes and then maybe go back at 18+ for University. I personally do not have any A Levels which I often think would be handy.

There are so many colleges now focusing on dance and musical theatre and they all offer more or less the same thing. Some have a bigger name than others. Some will specialise in just dance or maybe even just drama. Make sure you do your research and take a look around. Consider the travel options too as they are now all over the country. Will your child need to also find residence?

At 16 they can choose to do a BTEC, BA Hons or Diploma course or even a one year foundation course, which they can then top up afterwards.

There are various different funding opportunities for these including the DaDA (Dance and Drama Award) from the Government which helps with fees and living costs. These usually go to the top students who auditioned and will also look into family income.

Some 16+ Schools are State funded such as The Brit school in Croydon but again this can be very difficult to get into.

There will also be funding opportunities from the school itself but again these may only go to low income families.

Other options could be to crowd fund or look for a sponsor.

Once again, all colleges will have their own audition process. Some will hold an audition workshop day, others you will need to book in. Be aware of some asking for high fees just to audition so perhaps only choose your top five schools. A great way to look at some schools is to read the programmes at West End shows and see where some of the performers attended.

Universities can be applied via the normal UCAS route and a student loan can be applied for just like any other student would.

Some of the top Drama schools may only take a tiny number of students per year (RADA, LAMDA) so bare this in mind when applying as it will be tough competition.

Most Colleges/Universities will offer Agent showcases and various performance opportunities throughout the year too, so do make sure you look into what each place offers.

After Graduating from College/University, unfortunately not everyone is fortunate enough to walk into The West End but there are plenty of other jobs out there. Touring shows, Holiday parks, Cruise Ships, Immersive Theatre and gigging. Then to expand on performing there is teaching, casting, directing, producing, party entertainers, models, choreographers and plenty more. Everyone has to start somewhere. It isn't always about becoming famous or making loads of money. I have friends who have now become Personal Trainers and one friend who is now a Psychiatrist. With any degree you take you may then decide further down the line to have a career change and performing isn't any different. I sometimes wonder whether to retrain as a midwife! There are so many avenues available for 'The Future Performer.'

Kim's Top Tips for Singing

- Hydrate – Make sure you drink plenty of water, approximately 4 hours before a performance.
- No throat sweets, these are terrible for singers. If you have a sore throat, only drink water or lemon, honey and ginger (Hot). No throat sprays or any other gimmicks. All these do are hide the problem, they don't fix it!
- Exercise every day! I don't mean hitting the gym (Although of course this is great too) but use your vocal exercises to keep the muscles strong and engaged.
- Always learn new repertoire.

Self Tape Tips

- Find a quiet room/spot where you won't be disturbed
- Make sure you have a plain background behind you
- Make sure you have good lighting
- Always make sure it's landscape unless you're specifically asked for portrait
- Have someone else read in the other lines if necessary
- Always be off book
- Only do a slate if it is asked for
- A slate is usually delivered to the camera in your own accent with your name, age, height and location
- Always label the files correctly
- Read the instructions twice
- No makeup, hair dos or dressing up
- If you are using music, you will need another device to play this from. Don't have the music too loud or too near your phone so that it over powers any singing

Music and me

When I listen to music, I can be free.
I can dream and be anything I want to be.

When I hear the music, I feel so alive.
I believe it can help to not just survive.

When I sing with the music, I become me.
More than just existing, it fills me with glee.

When I play the music, it helps others too.
Helps them to smile and helps them be moved.

When I make music, it is more than just songs.
It is something that will stay with me all life long.

When I listen to music, the words become real.
It is more than just notes, it helps me to feel.

References

The AYPA – https://www.theaypa.co.uk
NNCEE - https://www.nncee.org.uk
KTTA - www.ktta.co.uk
Spotlight - https://www.spotlight.com/
The Stage - https://www.thestage.co.uk

@kimthursfieldvocal
@kttalentagency

Acknowledgments

Thank you to my parents who sent me to Stage School. Thank you to all parents whose children I teach or have taught over the years and to my lovely clients who I work with now. Thank you to my husband who put up with my ADHD brain whilst writing this book. Thank you to my best friend Sally who helped me with her advice. I love watching the journey of The Future Performer.

About the Author

Kim Thursfield is first a mother of two children. She trained at The Italia Conti Academy of Theatre Arts at The Barbican in London from the age of 12. After graduating at 18, she went into the big wide world of performing where she performed in Pantomimes, UK Tours, five star Hotels and some film and television programmes.

Once she married she had a full time job working in PR and Marketing for a Theatre where she learnt a lot about marketing a show, contacts, Producing and Directing including Producing and Directing her own show there for charity.

When Kim had her first daughter, she decided she didn't want to work full time and wanted to be freelance in order to work flexibly with family life.

She bought her own franchise Theatre School in Sevenoaks which she built from 0 – 85 students in three years. She then bought her second franchise school which was of equal success in only a year.

She ran her two schools alongside being a vocal coach for many top theatre schools in the area.

In 2018 one of her students landed a role in a Hollywood film. This then led her down the road of also building an agency.

Kim successfully sold both franchise schools and is now completely freelance working as a vocal coach and running her agency KTTA which has now seen many children and adults land roles in West End Musicals and TV/Film projects.

Kim still has many ideas for the future which included writing this book for other parents.

Kim is constantly passing on her industry knowledge to others and loves to see the success and happiness it can bring.

Printed in Great Britain
by Amazon